I0796223

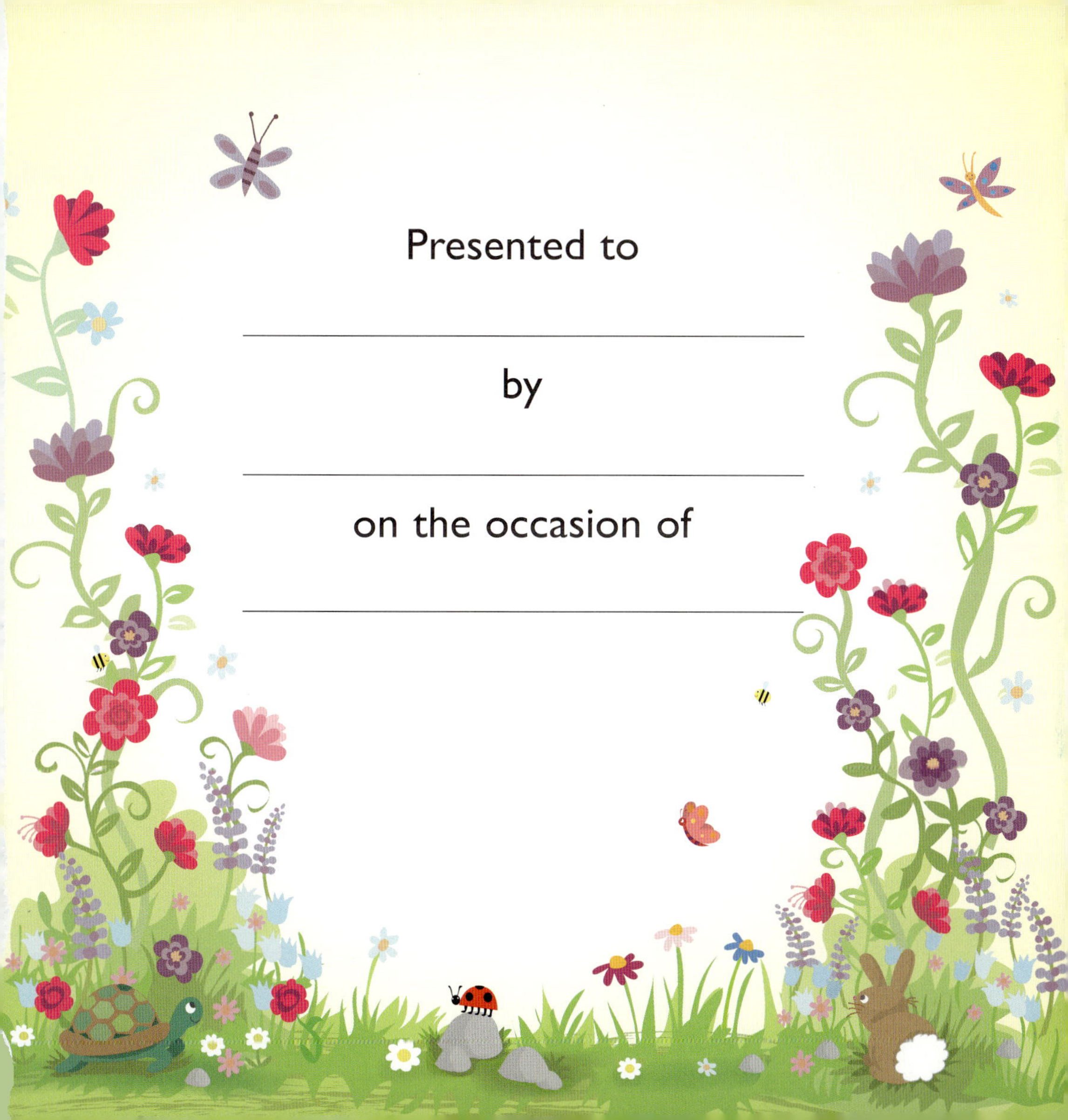

Presented to
by
on the occasion of

My Little BIBLE and PRAYERS

Karen Williamson
Illustrated by Amanda Enright

CANDLE BOOKS

Published by
Lion Hudson Limited
Wilkinson House, Jordan Hill Business Park,
Banbury Road, Oxford OX2 8DR, England
www.lionhudson.com

ISBN 978 1 78128 388 2

First published as *My Little Bible* in 2011, and *My Little Prayers* in 2013
First combined edition 2020

Acknowledgments
Every effort has been made to trace and contact copyright owners. We apologise for any inadvertent omissions or errors.

The Lord's Prayer on page 92 is adapted from the Good News Bible published by The Bible Societies/HarperCollins Publishers, copyright © 1966, 1971, 1976, 1992 American Bible Society.

All unattributed prayers by Karen Williamson are copyright © ZipAddress Limited

Psalm 23:1 (on page 206) is taken from The Authorized (King James) Version. Rights in the Authorized Version are vested in the Crown. Reproduced by permission of the Crown's patentee, Cambridge University Press.
The Lord's Prayer (on page 207) is adapted from the Holy Bible, New Living Translation, copyright © 1996, 2004, 2007 by Tyndale House Foundation. Used by permission of Tyndale House Publishers, Inc., Carol Stream, Illinois 60188. All rights reserved.

A catalogue record for this book is available from the British Library

Printed and bound in China, February 2020, LH54

Contents

The Story of God's People

Abram finds a new country

Long ago, in a far-off land called Ur, there lived a man named Abram.

One day God promised him, “I’m going to lead you to a special new country.”

"Look up!" God told Abram one night. "Can you count all the stars? One day there will be more people in your family than stars in the sky!"

Abram packed his bags and loaded up his animals. Abram and his relations left Ur. They set out for the special country that God had promised to Abram.

After journeying for many months, Abram came at last to the land that God had promised. There he settled down with his wife, Sarah.

Genesis 12, 13, 15:4–5

But Abram and Sarah were sad because they had no children. They had grown old, and there seemed no hope that they would ever have a baby.

One day God sent three messengers to visit Abram and Sarah. They said to Abram, "Your wife, Sarah, is going to have a son."

When she heard this, Sarah just laughed.

But, just as God had promised, a year later Sarah had a son. Abram and Sarah named him Isaac.

Genesis 15:1–4; 18:1–15; 21:1–7

After this, God changed Abram's name to Abraham – which means "father of many". And God gave Abraham great flocks of sheep and herds of camels.

Genesis 17:1–8

When he grew up, Isaac married a woman called Rebekah. They had twin sons, named Esau and Jacob. Esau loved to hunt wild animals. And Jacob, the younger of the two, was very crafty.

One day Jacob went to his old, blind father pretending he was Esau. Isaac was fooled by him. He gave Jacob the special blessing that should have been for his older son, Esau.

Esau was so furious that Jacob had to run away from home. He went far away to another country.

Genesis 25:19–27; 27:1–45

One night Jacob slept in the open, using a stone as a pillow. He had a beautiful dream. In his dream, he saw angels climbing up and down a stairway to heaven.

God promised Jacob, "I will always look after your family."

Genesis 28:10–22

Years later, Jacob returned to the Promised Land and made up with his brother, Esau.

Genesis 32–33

Jacob had a big family of twelve sons. He loved his young son, Joseph, most of all. Jacob gave Joseph a special coat. How smart he looked!

… And how jealous Joseph's brothers became!

They grew so angry that they took Joseph and sold him to traders. Then the brothers told Jacob that Joseph was dead. How Jacob wept!

Genesis 37:1–36

The traders took Joseph to Egypt, where he had lots of adventures. First he helped the captain of the king's guards, then he was thrown into jail. Finally Pharaoh, king of Egypt, made Joseph his top minister!

One year, no rain fell. No one could find enough to eat.

But in Egypt, Joseph had saved up plenty of grain in great storehouses.

Genesis 39–41

When old Jacob heard of this, he took his family to Egypt to find food. What a wonderful surprise it was to discover his son Joseph was alive!

Genesis 42–47

Escape from Egypt!

So Joseph's family settled in Egypt. They were called "Hebrews" and grew in number.

Years later, a new Pharaoh ruled Egypt. He made the Hebrews work very hard for him.

Pharaoh worried that there were too many Hebrews. "Kill every Hebrew baby boy!" he commanded.

Exodus 1

But one Hebrew mother hid her baby in a basket. Then she floated the basket in the river.

Pharaoh's daughter, the princess of Egypt, found the baby in the basket.

She took the child to her royal palace. He was safe!

The princess of Egypt brought him up as a royal prince. She named him "Moses".

Exodus 2:1–10

When Moses grew up, he ran away from Egypt. He went to live as a shepherd in the desert.

One day an angel spoke to Moses from a burning bush.

"Go back to Egypt," said the angel. "Tell Pharaoh 'Let my people go!'"

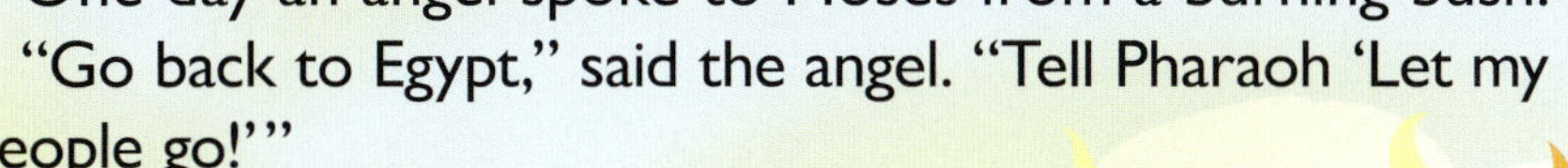

Exodus 2:11–23; 3

Moses was very frightened. But he went to Pharaoh time after time, telling him, “Let my people go!”

At long last Pharaoh gave in.

“Go – and take your people with you!” he shouted.

In a great hurry, the Hebrews prepared to leave Egypt. They set out for the land that God had promised Abraham.

Exodus 7–12

It wasn't long before Pharaoh changed his mind. He chased after the Hebrews.

But when the king of Egypt came to the Red Sea, he and his soldiers were drowned. God had already helped Moses get his people safely across.

Exodus 14

The Hebrews lived in the desert many years. God gave them special food called "manna". But they often grumbled and complained. They even made a golden statue and danced around it, instead of praying to God!

Exodus 16, 32

One day, Moses climbed a high mountain. When he came down, he was carrying two great stones. On them were written God's rules for everyone. We call them the "Ten Commandments".

Exodus 20

God instructed his people to build a really big tent, where the priests could pray to God.

When the Hebrews moved on, they packed up the tent and carried it with them.

Exodus 26

In the Promised Land

Moses sent out spies to explore the land God had promised them. Two spies came back saying, "It's a land full of fruit and other good food."

The rest came back saying it would be very dangerous to enter the Promised Land.

Numbers 13

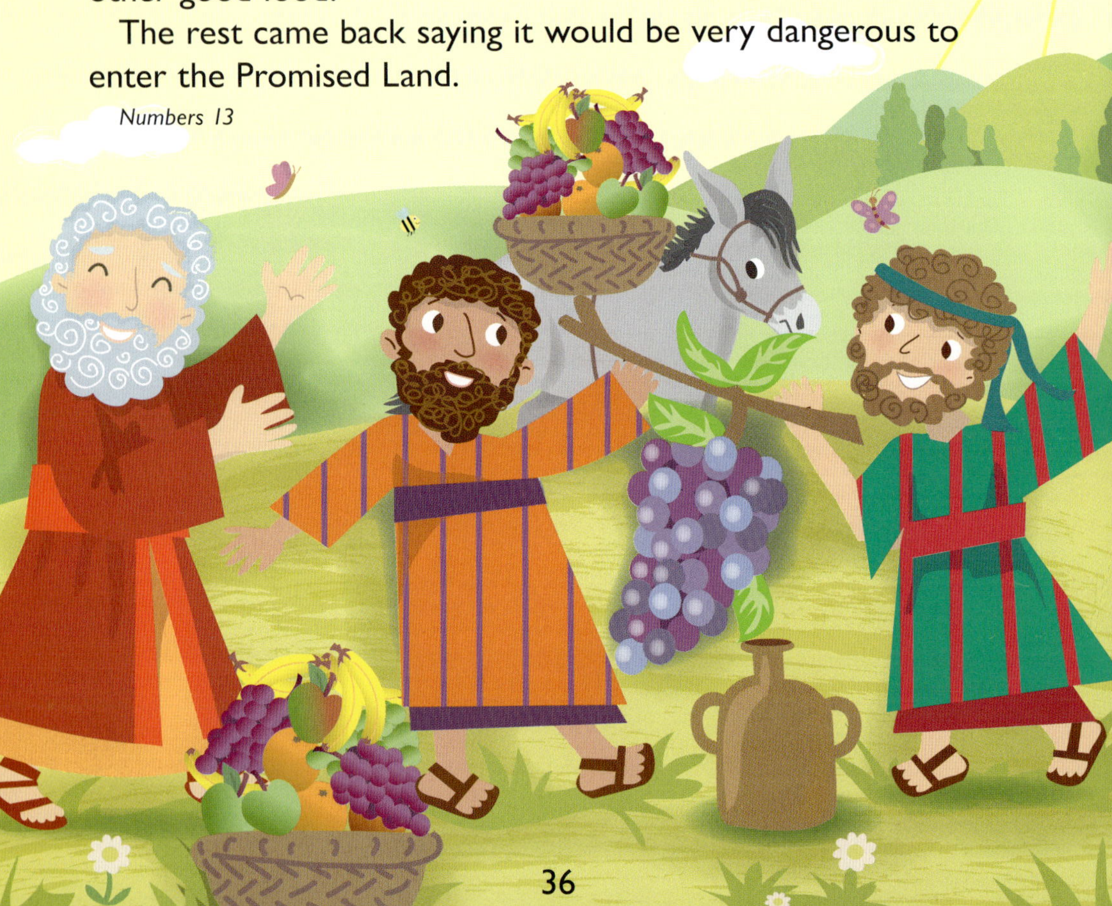

After many years, Moses died. God's people crossed the River Jordan and entered the Promised Land. But they still had to capture it.

Joshua 3–4

God gave special orders for capturing the great city of Jericho. The people walked around and around it. Then, when the priests blew their trumpets and the people shouted, the city walls collapsed!

Joshua 5:13 – 6:27

God's people became known as the Israelites. God gave them special new leaders.

One great leader was called Gideon. With God's help, Gideon defeated their enemies.

Gideon attacked at night, with flaming torches and lots of blaring trumpets! The enemy were sleeping in their tents. They ran away terrified.

Judges 7

But God's people weren't content.

"Give us a king!" they demanded. "Every other nation has a king."

1 Samuel 8

Kings for Israel

So God told a priest named Samuel to find a man fit to be king of Israel.

God helped Samuel find a man called Saul.

Samuel poured a little oil on Saul's head to show that God had chosen him to become king.

1 Samuel 9–10

At first Saul ruled well. But later, he disobeyed God and did wrong things.

So God sent Samuel off to find a new king.

1 Samuel 15

Samuel visited the home of a man called Jesse, who had many sons. Jesse paraded his sons before Samuel. But none of them seemed right to become king of Israel.

“Do you have any more sons?” asked Samuel.

“Well, there’s young David,” Jesse answered. “But he’s only a shepherd boy.”

“Send for him!” said Samuel. “Perhaps he’s the one God wants.”

They brought David in from the fields. He was handsome and glowing with health.

At once Samuel knew God had chosen David to become the next king of Israel.

1 Samuel 16:1–13

David was very bold.

He killed the giant Goliath – the enemy of Israel – with a single stone from his sling.

1 Samuel 17

David became a great king. He beat his nation's enemies.

David also loved to play on his harp and sing about God's love. He wrote many songs of his own.

David made the city of Jerusalem his capital. Later, he brought the special box containing the Ten Commandments into Jerusalem. He was so happy that he danced in front of it.

2 Samuel 6

When David died, his son Solomon became king of Israel. Solomon was a very wise ruler.

1 Kings 2

When people had a problem, they came to Solomon and asked him what to do.

1 Kings 3

The queen of Sheba lived far away. She journeyed for many days just to hear Solomon's wise sayings.

1 Kings 10:1–13

King Solomon built a wonderful new temple in Jerusalem.

It was made of the best wood, stone, and gold. Priests led prayer and worship there.

1 Kings 6

The people turn away from God

But after Solomon died, the people began to disobey God's laws.

The kingdom split in two. One part was called Judah, the other part Israel.

God sent his people special messengers, called prophets. They told the people to return to God's way. The prophet Elijah warned wicked King Ahab.

"Worship the living God," Elijah told Ahab.

Elijah built a great heap of stones. Then he prayed. God sent fire from heaven onto the stones.

1 Kings 17–18

God sent many other prophets.

A prophet named Jeremiah warned that God would let enemies attack if his people didn't turn back to God.

God sent a prophet named Jonah to warn people in the city of Nineveh to mend their ways. But Jonah got scared and jumped aboard a ship going the other way!

A great storm arose, and the sailors threw Jonah overboard.

But God sent a great fish that swallowed Jonah. Three days later the fish spat him up on a beach.

After this, Jonah was ready to do what God had told him to do.

Jonah 1–3

God sent many other prophets. Isaiah, Daniel, and a shepherd named Amos.

They warned the Israelites, "Mend your ways – or God will send enemies to attack and punish you."

But still God's people didn't listen.

So cruel kings came from the countries of Assyria and Babylon and carried off the Israelites. They even destroyed the city of Jerusalem.

2 Kings 25

But the prophets had words of hope for God's people too.

"God still loves you," they promised. "He will send a special person to save you."

Many years later, that special person came – just as God had promised.

His name was Jesus.

Jesus of Nazareth

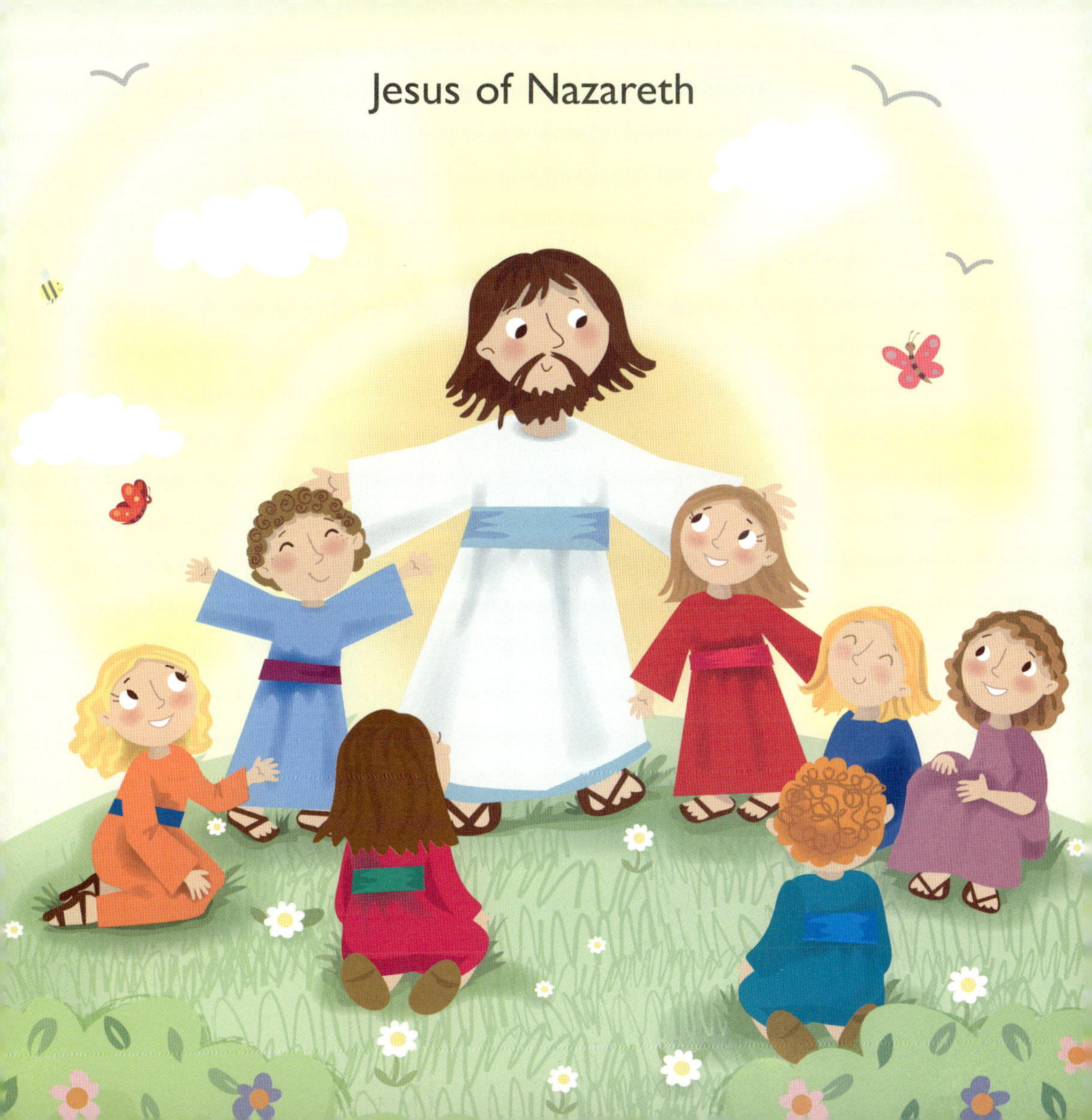

The very first Christmas

In the town of Nazareth there lived a young woman called Mary.

One day, the angel Gabriel appeared to Mary.

"You are going to have a very special baby," he said. "You must call him Jesus."

Luke 1:26–38

Mary went to visit her cousin Elizabeth.

"I'm going to have a baby boy," Mary told her. Elizabeth was expecting a baby too. His name was to be John. Both women were very happy.

Luke 1:39–45

Mary married Joseph the carpenter.

Just before her baby was due, they had to make a long journey to Bethlehem. Mary was very tired when they reached the town.

Bethlehem was full of visitors.
Mary and Joseph couldn't find anywhere to sleep.

Then a kind innkeeper said, “You can stay in my stable.” Mary and Joseph accepted gratefully.

There, in the little stable in Bethlehem, Jesus was born. The donkeys and cows watched quietly.

Mary cuddled the newborn baby. Then she laid him to sleep on straw in the animals' manger.

Luke 2:1–7

Shepherds were sleeping in fields near Bethlehem.

Suddenly they saw a bright light and then an angel appeared.

"Tonight a child is born in Bethlehem," announced the angel. "He has come to save his people."

The shepherds rushed off at once to find the newborn baby. When they came to the stable, they knelt before baby Jesus.

Luke 2:8–20

Far away in a distant land, some wise men noticed a special star in the sky. "Let us follow the star and find the newborn baby," they said.

After a long, long journey, the wise men arrived at the little town of Bethlehem.

There the star stopped.

When the wise men saw Jesus, they knelt before him.

They brought him rich gifts: gold, precious frankincense, and perfume called myrrh.

Matthew 2:1–12

Jesus and his family

Mary and Joseph took Jesus back home to Nazareth.

There Jesus grew up. He helped Joseph in his carpenter's yard and played with his friends. He helped Mary in the house.

Matthew 2:19–23

When Jesus was twelve, he visited Jerusalem with his parents for a special holiday.

But Mary and Joseph lost Jesus among the crowds.

At last they found him again. Jesus was talking to the Jewish teachers in the Temple.

Mary and Joseph were astonished at the wise things Jesus was telling them.

Luke 2:41–52

When Jesus grew up, he worked with Joseph as a carpenter.

But he knew God had a special job for him to do.

This map shows the land where Jesus lived.
MOUNT HERMON
GALILEE
Capernaum
Lake Galilee
Nazareth
SAMARIA
River Jordan
Jericho
JUDEA
Jerusalem
Bethlehem

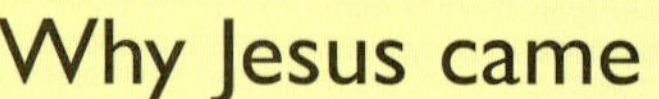

Why Jesus came

Jesus' cousin, John, started to preach beside the River Jordan.

He told people to turn away from the bad things they were doing.

John dipped them in the river to show they wanted to make a clean start.

One day Jesus came to the river. "Please baptize me, too," he said to John.

But John said, "You are the good one: you should baptize me!"

But Jesus insisted. So John dipped Jesus in the river. As Jesus came out of the water, God spoke like thunder. "This is my son," he said. "I'm very pleased with him!"

Matthew 3:1–17

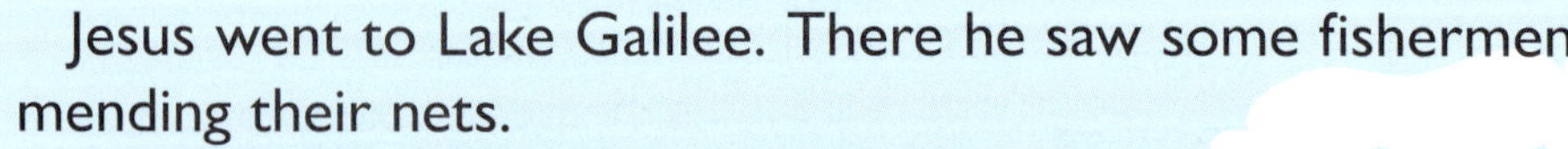

Jesus went to Lake Galilee. There he saw some fishermen mending their nets.

"Follow me," he said.

And straightaway the men left their nets and followed Jesus. Their names were Simon Peter and his brother Andrew; James and his brother John.

These men became some of Jesus' special friends.

Jesus also invited some other men to become his special followers. He called Matthew the taxman, Thomas the twin, another James, Philip, Bartholomew, Simon, Judas Iscariot, and another Judas.

Altogether Jesus had twelve special friends. Sometimes we call them Jesus' "disciples" or "apostles".

Mark 1:14–20; Luke 6:12–16

One of his friends said, "Jesus, teach us to pray."
So Jesus said, "When you pray, say:

'Our Father in heaven,
Holy is your name;
May your kingdom come.
May your will
be done here on earth
just as it is in heaven.
Give us today
the food we need.
Forgive us the wrong we have done,
as we forgive those
who have wronged us.
Do not bring us to hard testing,
but keep us safe from evil.
Amen.'"

Matthew 6:9–15

Jesus and his friends started walking to nearby towns and villages. Jesus told people there special stories about how God wants our world to be. People were amazed when they heard him talk.

Jesus told this story about a shepherd with 100 sheep:

"One day one of the sheep got lost. So the shepherd left the 99 and went out to search for his lost sheep.

"After looking everywhere, at last the shepherd found the lost sheep and carried it home on his shoulders. The shepherd was so happy to find the lost sheep."

Jesus said, "God is just as happy as the shepherd when anyone turns away from doing bad things."

Luke 15:1–7

Jesus told another story:

"A man was walking from Jerusalem to Jericho when he was set upon by thieves. A priest went past without helping. Then a worker from the Temple went past without helping.

"Finally a stranger from the land of Samaria came along. He did stop to help the injured man. Then he took him to an inn and paid for him to be looked after."

"Which of the three passers-by was a true friend?" Jesus asked.

"The man who helped," said his listeners.

"You go and do the same," said Jesus.

Luke 10:25–37

Many sick people came to Jesus.

People with bad backs and bad legs.

People who couldn't see and people who couldn't hear.

Jesus healed them all.

A man called Jairus came to Jesus.

"My daughter is very ill," he said. "Please make her better."

But by the time Jesus reached Jairus's house, the little girl had died.

Jesus took her hand. "Little girl," he said. "Get up!" Jairus's daughter got up at once and had something to eat.

Luke 8:40–56

Jesus did other miracles too.

One day, he fed 5,000 people with just five loaves and two fish!

Luke 9:10–17

Another time, Jesus went sailing on Lake Galilee with his friends, the disciples. He fell asleep in the boat.

A storm suddenly arose and the disciples were afraid the boat would sink.

They woke Jesus.

"Quick! Help us!" they cried. "Or we'll all drown!"

Jesus said to the storm: "Peace! Be still!"
And at once the wind dropped and the sea was calm.

Luke 8:22–25

Jesus returns to Jerusalem

Jesus decided to travel to Jerusalem.

"I'm going to die soon," he told his disciples.

They were sad. They didn't understand what he meant.

Some of the people in Jerusalem hated Jesus.
"He doesn't keep our laws," they said.
So they were plotting to kill him.

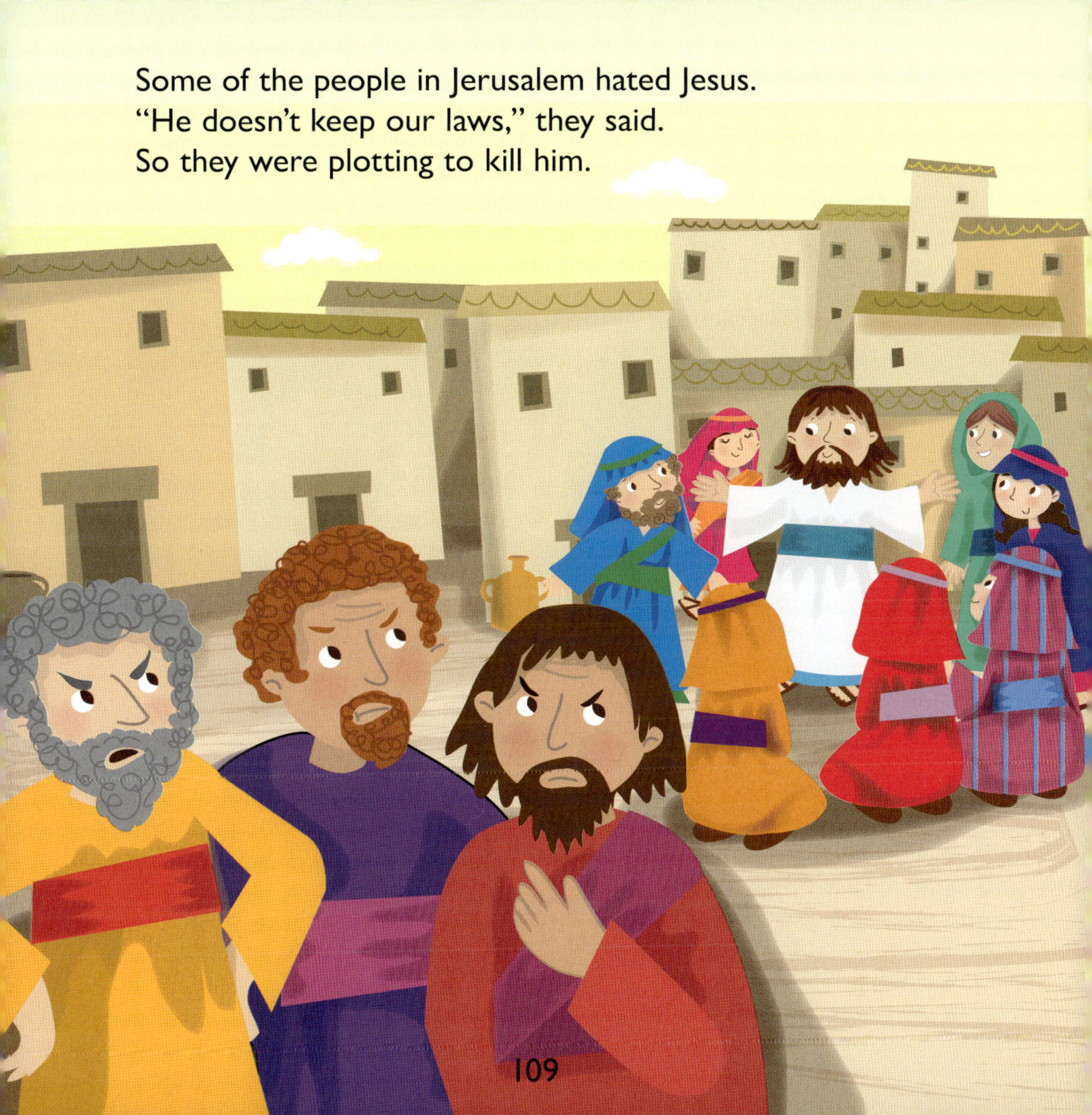

Judas, one of Jesus' own followers, turned against him. He plotted with Jesus' enemies.

Luke 22:1–6

Jesus arrived in Jerusalem at festival time.

"May I borrow a donkey?" he asked. "I would like to ride into the city."

When people saw him coming, they waved palm branches.
"Jesus is our King!" they shouted.
They threw their cloaks on the ground.

Luke 19:28–38; John 12:12–16

One night, Jesus ate a special supper with his disciples.
"I'm going to die soon," he told them again.
But they still didn't understand why he said this.

Jesus took bread and poured wine.

"Every time you eat bread or drink wine," he said, "remember me."

Then Jesus took his disciples out into a garden. There Jesus prayed to his heavenly Father. But all the disciples fell asleep.

Matthew 26:17–46

The very first Easter

While Jesus was in the garden, Judas led Jesus' enemies to him. Jesus' disciples were very frightened and ran away.

Soldiers marched Jesus off to the Roman ruler.
Jesus' enemies said, "Jesus has broken our law."
But the ruler said, "This man has done *nothing* wrong!"

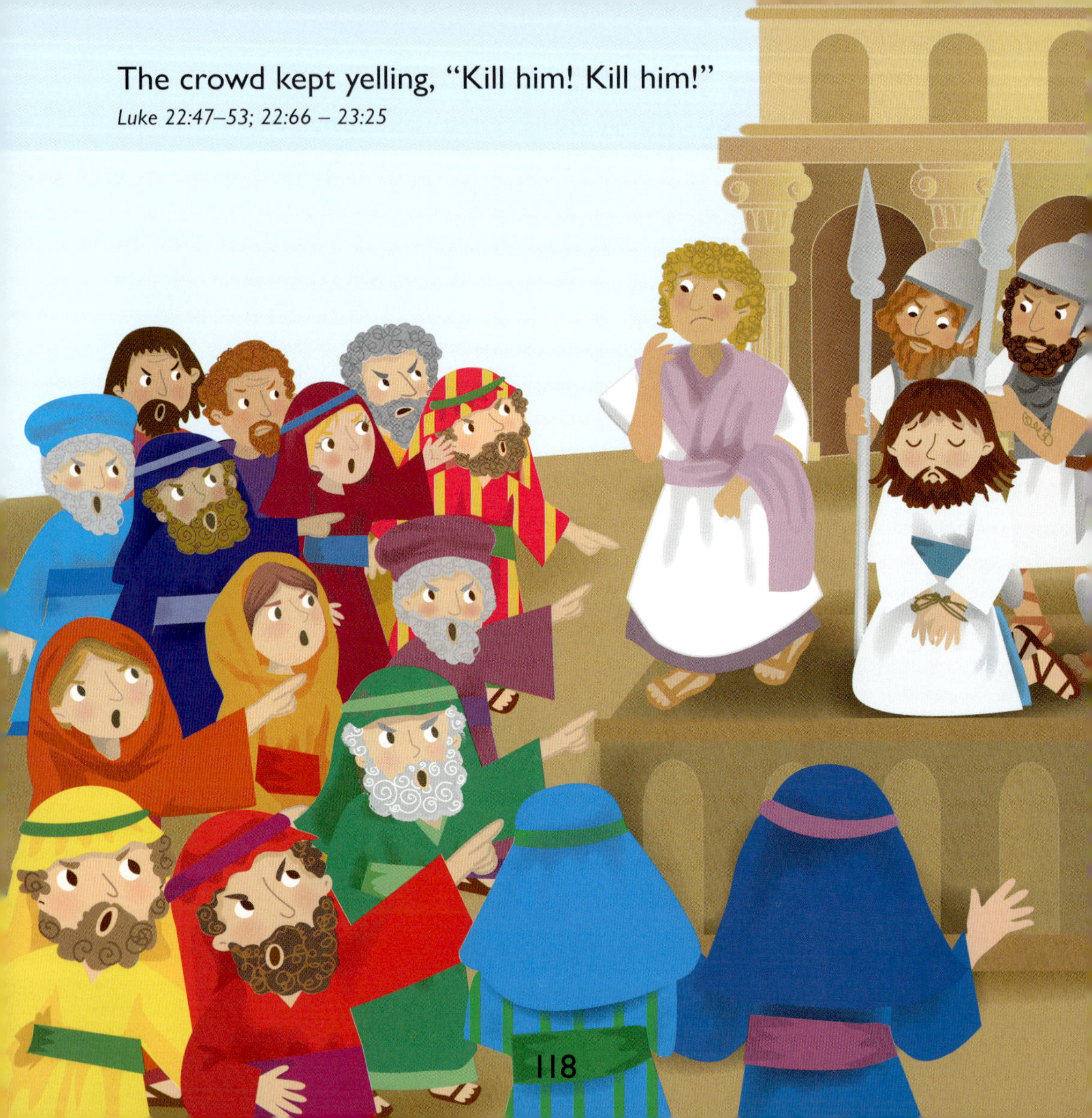

The crowd kept yelling, “Kill him! Kill him!”

Luke 22:47–53; 22:66 – 23:25

So cruel soldiers marched Jesus away.
They took him outside the city.
There they put him to death on a wooden cross.

Luke 23:26–46

Jesus' followers were very sad.
They had lost a very special person.

Friends laid Jesus' body in a cave. Then they rolled a great stone across the doorway.

Matthew 27:57–60

Two days later, Jesus' friends Peter and John came to visit his tomb. The stone had been rolled away!

They were astonished – and a bit scared.

Jesus is alive!

Then Peter and John looked into the tomb.
There was no body!
Then they knew Jesus had risen from the dead.

Peter and John rushed off to tell the rest of Jesus' disciples what they had seen.

Later, Jesus appeared to them all in a room in Jerusalem.

John 20:1–9, 19–20

Soon after, some disciples went fishing on Lake Galilee.

They saw Jesus on the beach. He was cooking breakfast for them.

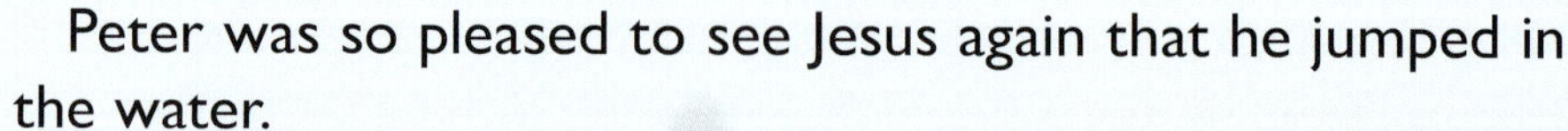

Peter was so pleased to see Jesus again that he jumped in the water.

John 21:1–14

Not long after this, Jesus left his friends.
He returned to his heavenly Father.
But the disciples knew that Jesus was alive forever.

Luke 24:50–53

Jesus promised: "One day I will return as king!"

My Little PRAYERS

Contents

Praise God!

Dear God,
I feel like praising you.
I like singing to you at the
top of my voice!
Thank you for everything!

Give me joy in my heart,
Keep me praising,
Give me joy in my heart, I pray;
Give me joy in my heart,
Keep me praising
Till the break of day.

Traditional

Praise him, praise him,
Everybody praise him –
God is love, God is love!

Traditional

A new day!

Dear Lord Jesus,
We have this day only once.
Before it goes,
help us to do the good we can,
so it's not wasted.

At school

Dear Lord,
I am starting my new school tomorrow.
I'm really scared.
There are big butterflies in my tummy.
Please come to school with me
and help me make new friends.
Thank you, Lord.

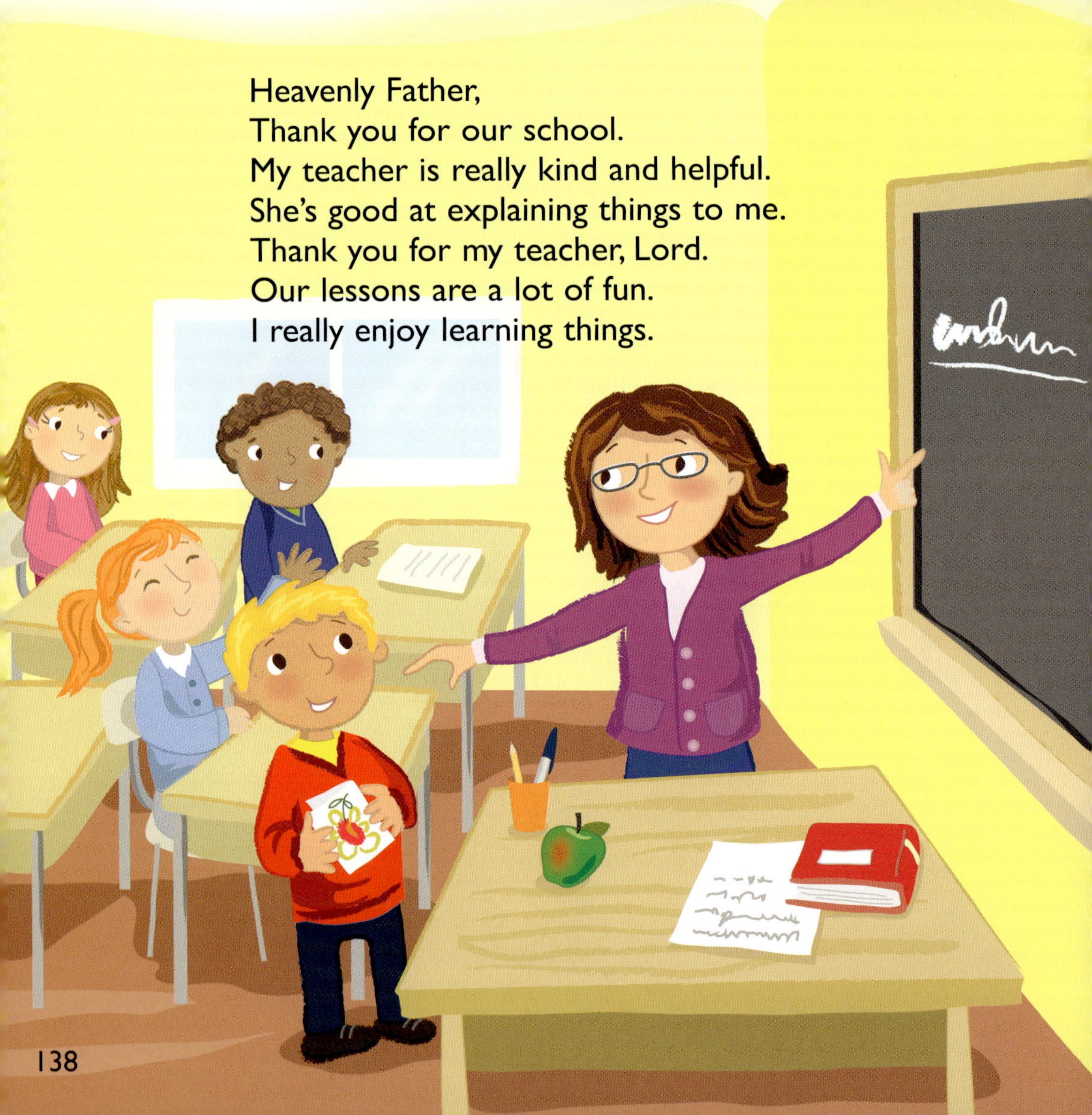

Heavenly Father,
Thank you for our school.
My teacher is really kind and helpful.
She's good at explaining things to me.
Thank you for my teacher, Lord.
Our lessons are a lot of fun.
I really enjoy learning things.

Dear Jesus,
Please help me at school.
Sometimes I find it hard,
and then I specially need you to help me.
Amen

Dear Lord Jesus,
Please help me to be brave.
I'm scared of lots of things.
I'm scared of big boys in the playground.
I'm scared of our friends' dog.
Please take away my fears.
Thank you, God.

Dinner time

Thank you for the world so sweet,
Thank you for the food we eat,
Thank you for the birds that sing,
Thank you, God, for everything.

Edith Rutter-Leatham (1870–1939)

Heavenly Father,
Thank you for our daily food.
Our tummies are always full!
Please help the poor children we see on TV
who don't get enough to eat every day.

God is great, God is good.
Let us thank him for our food.
By his hands, we are fed.
Let us thank him for our bread.
Amen

Traditional

God, we thank you for this food,
For rest and home and all things good;
For wind and rain and sun above,
But most of all for those we love.

Thank you

God made the sun,
God made the trees,
God made the mountains,
And God made me.

Thank you, God,
For the sun and the trees,
For making the mountains,
And for making me.

Dear Lord,
Thank you for music.
I love hearing happy songs
– and singing them, too.
Thank you for giving us music,
Lord.

Hooray!
You made the giraffe as tall as a tree.
Thank you, God.
Hooray!
You made the caterpillar, ant, and bee.
Thank you, God.
Hooray!
You made our world so perfectly.
Thank you, God.

Dear God,
Thank you for giving us the Bible,
so we can learn about you.
Amen

Dear God,
You know all about me.
You know the colour of my eyes.
You know what I most like to eat.
You know when I'm happy or sad.
And you know what's best for me.
Thank you, Lord.

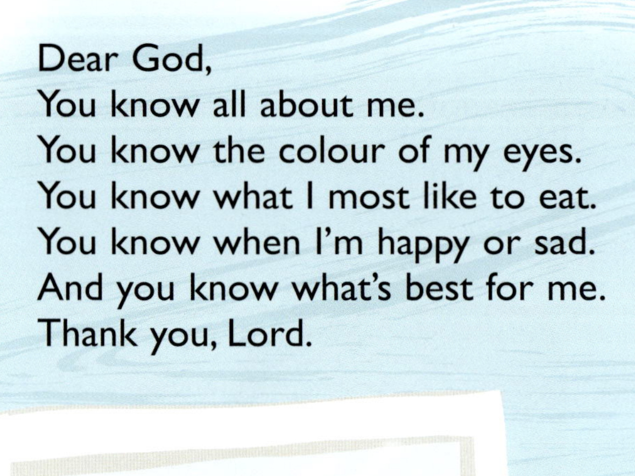

Dear Lord,
I saw a beautiful rainbow this afternoon.
It made me remember the story of Noah
and the Flood.
Thank you for the rainbow, Lord.

Travels

Dear Lord,
We're off on a trip tomorrow.
I'm so excited.
Thank you for holidays!

Dear Lord,
I'm glad that, even when we're far from home,
you're still with us.
Please keep us safe.
Amen

Quiet times

Hush little puppy with your bow wow wow,
Hush little kitty with your meow, meow, meow.
Hush Mr Rooster with your cock-a-doodle-doo.
Don't you moo moo moo, Mrs Cow.
Hush, hush, hush.
Hush, hush, hush.
Somebody's talking to God right now.

Traditional

Dear Lord Jesus,
Thank you for prayer time.
Thank you that we can talk to you about
anything,
anytime,
anywhere.

Dear God,
Thank you that
– with you –
I'm never alone.
Amen

Dear God,
Thank you that we can tell you our secrets:
things that make us happy;
things we worry about;
things we look forward to;
things we're scared of.
We can share all of them with you.
Thank you, Lord.

Please, God

God, make my life a little light
Within this world to glow;
A little flame that burns so bright
Wherever I may go.

Matilda Betham-Edwards (1836–1919)

Heavenly Father,
Guard my little tongue today,
Make it kind while I play;
Keep my hands from doing wrong,
Guide my feet all day long.

Dear Lord, thank you!
You answered my prayer!
Things went all right today.
You really helped me, Lord.
Next time I won't feel so frightened.

My friend Jesus

Jesus, friend of little children,
Be a friend to me;
Take my hand and ever keep me,
Close to thee.

Walter J. Mathams (1851–1931)

With all that I do,
And all that I say,
Help me to walk
In Jesus' way.

When I'm scared...

Dear Lord,
Sometimes I get lonely.
I'm too shy to talk to anyone.
I feel left out.
Please help me fit in and make friends.
I know you will always be my friend.
Thank you, Lord.

All the people I love

God bless all those I love;
God bless all those who love me;
God bless all those who love those I love,
And all those who love those who love me.

From an old New England sampler

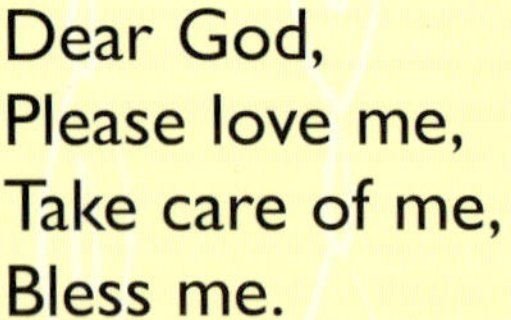

Dear God,
Please love me,
Take care of me,
Bless me.

Please love my sister,
Take care of her,
Bless her.

Please love my brother,
Take care of him,
Bless him.

Dear Lord Jesus,
Thank you for cuddles.
Thank you for hugs and kisses.

Dear Lord, thank you
for giving me so much love.
Amen

Dear Lord Jesus,
I love my mummy and daddy.
I love my brother and sister.
I love my grandma and grandpa.
Please look after them.
Please don't forget to look after me too, Lord!

Dear Lord,
Great news!
My new baby sister is here at last.
She looks very small.
Her fingers are tiny.
I can't wait to play with her.
Please help her grow up fast, so I can.

Dear Heavenly Father,
Please bring my parents
Safely home from work.
Thank you for
Goodnight hugs.

Dear Lord,
Sometimes my brother makes
me cross.
I get fed up with him.
Please help me love my brother
and get on better with him.

God's wonderful world

For air and sunshine, pure and sweet,
We thank our heavenly Father;
For grass that grows beneath our feet,
We thank our heavenly Father.

Traditional

Lord God,
You provide streams of water
in the hills and valleys.
Birds build their nests nearby
and sing in the trees.
With all my heart
I praise you, Lord!

Dear Lord,
Today we went to the zoo.
We saw lots of animals you made.
Giant elephants, whizzy lizards,
mischievous monkeys, gentle deer.
You made them all, God,
big and small.

Thank you, Lord Jesus,
For all the plants and animals
You've given us to share –
From the yellow daffodil,
To the grizzly bear.

Sorry!

Dear Lord,
I'm sorry I was so naughty today.
Please forgive me.
Sometimes I find it hard to be good.
Please help me to be nicer tomorrow.

Lord, please forgive me.
Today I was unkind to my friend.
Help her to forgive me
when I tell her I'm sorry.

God, you are great.
You made the world and it's so good.
We're sorry that we have spoiled it.
Please help us to do better.
Amen

Children, everywhere
For lonely children everywhere,
Who don't have anyone to care;
Lord, I pray that you will send
A loving, kind, and special friend.
Author unknown

Lord Jesus,
Please make my friend well.
Help the doctors and nurses
make her better.
Amen

Birthdays

Thank you, Lord,
For people and parties,
For presents and cards,
For songs and games.
Thank you for cakes and candles.
Thank you for birthdays, Lord.

Dear Lord,
I had the best birthday party ever.
All my friends came.
They gave me lots of cards and presents.
I blew out all the candles on my cake in one puff.
Thank you for a wonderful birthday.

Harvest

All good gifts around us
Are sent from heaven above.
Then thank the Lord,
O thank the Lord,
For all his love.

Matthias Claudius (1740–1815)

Now thank we all our God
With hearts and hands and voices;
Such wonders he has done,
In him his world rejoices.

Martin Rinkart (1586–1649)

Christmas

Loving Father,
Help us remember the birth of Jesus,
So we may join in the song of the angels,
Share the gladness of the shepherds,
And worship with the wise men.

Adapted from a prayer by Robert Louis Stevenson (1850-94)

What can I give him,
Poor as I am?
If I were a shepherd,
I would give a lamb;
If I were a wise man,
I would do my part;
Yet what I can I give him –
Give my heart

Christina Rossetti (1830–94)

Easter

There is a green hill far away,
Outside a city wall,
Where the dear Lord was crucified
Who died to save us all.

Lord God, we thank you for your love,
shown to us in Jesus Christ,
who was willing to die for us.

Cecil Frances Alexander (1818–94)

Loving heavenly Father,
We thank you for the new life
that we celebrate at Easter.
Amen

At the end of the day

Hello God! It's me!
What a great day it's been.
Did you see everything I did today?
Of course – because you're God!
Thanks for being with me.

Dear God,
I did something wrong today.
You know what it was, God.

I'm sorry.
Please forgive me.
Thank you, God.

Dear God,
Did you hear me crying today?
I was sad.
Thank you for listening
When I'm not so happy.

Heavenly Father,
Sometimes I get cross inside,
and have a bad mood day.
I scream and shout and stamp my feet,
if I don't get my way.

I'm sorry for my bad mood, Lord.
I'm glad that, whether I'm good or bad,
You love me anyway.

Lord Jesus,
Thank you for everything good that happened today:
For keeping me safe and well.
For fun with friends,
For what I learned,
For those I love.
Help me to sleep safely tonight.
Amen

Dear God,
Tomorrow is a very important day for me.
You know about it.
Please look after me tomorrow.
Thank you for listening, God.
I am not so worried now.

Bedtime

Matthew, Mark, Luke, and John,
Bless the bed that I lie on.
Four corners to my bed,
Four angels around my head.

Traditional

Dear Lord,
I like it when I lie in bed at night
and listen to the wind and rain.
I feel cosy and safe.
Thank you for my snuggly, warm bed.
Please look after all the animals
outside in the cold.
Find them somewhere safe and warm.

Dear Lord Jesus,
Please look after me at bedtime.
Sometimes I wake up in the middle of the night
and feel scared.
Help me to remember you are always with me
and that I don't need to be afraid.
I'm glad you're my friend.

As night-time comes creeping,
And children are sleeping,
God watches us, deep through the night.

So hush now, no peeping,
For God will be keeping
Us safe, till the new morning's light.

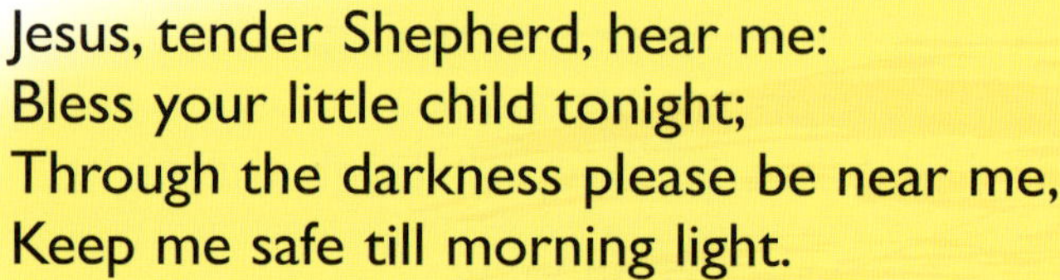

Jesus, tender Shepherd, hear me:
Bless your little child tonight;
Through the darkness please be near me,
Keep me safe till morning light.

All this day your hand has led me,
And I thank you for your care;
You have warmed me, clothed and fed me;
Listen to my evening prayer.

Mary Lundie Duncan (1814–40)

Through the night

If I wake afraid
From scary thoughts and fears,
May I know, Lord,
That you are near.

The Lord is my shepherd;
I shall not want.
Amen

The Lord's Prayer

Our Father in heaven,
May your name be kept holy.
May your kingdom come soon.
May your will be done here on earth,
just as it is in heaven.
Give us our food for today,
and forgive us our sins,
just as we forgive those who sin against us.
And don't let us yield to temptation,
but deliver us from the evil one.
For yours is the kingdom, the power,
And the glory,
For ever and ever,
Amen

An old prayer

God be in my head,
And in my understanding;
God be in my eyes,
And in my looking;
God be in my mouth,
And in my speaking;
God be in my heart,
And in my thinking.

Sarum Primer (1527)